JAH ELLIOT

Unchained

Inside the mind of a psycho

Contents

I

The Unknown

In life, there will always be things of the unknown. Some things are so unknown nothing can express or convey what they mean, their origin, or their purpose. Also, the unknown is more so metaphysical. It consists of more than just things of the world but a divine presence in nature. The unknown raises questions of something greater than what can be seen, heard, or felt. The unknown is the why of everything known. But once the unknown is known, the known becomes unknown.

1

The Devil Enjoying Freedom

The devil is always depicted as a mammoth hideous creature with horns and monstrous features. This is not the case the devil is gorgeous, smooth, and angelic. But most people tend to forget God created the devil in a sense.

The devil chose to overrule God and exalt himself to heaven which brought evil into the universe. The devil's very own will turned him against God. The devil wanted his own will, land, followers, and throne. Not just the devil of Christ but the mortal devil's who walk among men. A devil can take many forms and with the depiction of the devil being misconstrued, we often miss the devils who are apparent.

The devil of this story is Cathey Milton who explains her life story aloud at an abandoned park to herself as she holds a mirror directly in her face. Although she is talking to herself her voice is heard over many miles as well as her story. But I will explain her story as if it were told directly to me through the *Jaheism* art form.

2

The Only Home I Have Ever Known

Through my thirty-four years of living, I have traveled almost the whole world. "You see Cathey!? Look at where I am now! Still traveling the world. But this world is nothing like the world I was born in, nor like my home, this home is the realm inside my head. Everything is perfect there. I'm perfect, the people are perfect, the environment is perfect, the rules and norms are perfect and my actions whether they are good or bad never suffer consequences. The perfect universe. I wish people could see my world and live gracefully in it. Everyone would be so happy in a world where everything is yours except the things I own and created which everything. People would live in a world of "nothing" since there is nothing the purpose of your life and existence solely depends upon me. I can create life, end life, cause wars, and confusion, create peace, end wars, and mostly destroy my universe and create a new one.

The things of the world around me do not even matter. Because I have no control over anything except myself. Or do I? But what I find so peculiar about the world around us is it can never be perfect nor will it ever be. "So why should I exemplify perfection in an imperfect world?" I asked myself that question every day I became conscious of my life and this world. Cathey, you are a genius! I know. But the people of this world think I'm a psychopath. "Why do they think that Cathey?" I do not know maybe because I talk to myself crazily, or because I look crazy, or some of the things I may do when I'm living in my world people of this world do not understand. Fuck em! In my head, everything I see is true because it comes from me and is only seen by me. It's not meant for others. If everyone can see it no one can see it all. I tell myself that too. It makes sense to me. "Cathey?" "Yes?" "Remember what mom would always ask?" Oh yeah. She used to always ask me, "Cathey when are you coming back home?" I always told her, "I'm already home so basically I'm never coming back." She always ranted when I told her I was never coming back home but it was for the best of us. I loved her dearly such a sweet woman but our worlds never coincided so I felt that I needed to live in my own home where my thoughts, ideas, feelings, and emotions were my very own. My mom always tried to control me in any way she could. She was always like that because she lived in her own world as well but her world matched the reality everyone else lives in. That's a tragedy written all over.

I feel if anything is going to be a tragedy I need to be the one causing it and not receiving it. That's why I chose to live in my world instead of hers. Every time something happens big or small it always ended miserably. Especially in my mom's world. If did not do a specific chore, my homework, or do what she said not to do she would beat me, starve me, burn me, strangle me, and sometimes tied me to a chair in a corner and call me out my name. This was an everyday thing even if nothing is wrong she find something and punish me for it even if it was her mistake.

Not only would she punish me but the punishment would last weeks or months. She would even sit me down in front of her and say, "You are a fucking whore!" Or say, "You are no more than me" for hours at a time and then force me to sleep.

At times as the punishment prolonged, it would get so bad to where I lied to myself and told myself, "Cathey this is a normal mom just wants you to get used to it." So I took every punishment as if I deserved it. After the punishment was over I would go into my room and fantasize about a life in my head that one day I would create. A life where I'm the ruler giving out punishment and seeking those who did without my permission and punishing them. The same as mom did but worse. That's how I know not crazy that's what I was taught.

A home is a place of comfort, relaxation, joy, and peace. All of that is subjective to every homeowner but I find peace in giving others peace. Death I should say. A form of peace where everything is uplifted more importantly the soul of those who is brought peace. All I ever wanted was peace and I was going to get it even if I had to give someone a piece of me. Which I did wholeheartedly.

Once I chose a life of peace many things started to change including my home life. I also understood peace is a sense of self so I need to find it within. So one day I asked my mom, "Are you peaceful?" She said, "The only way there will be peace is if I'm dead. I'm not dead yet so there will never be peace around here." My soul was eager once I heard her say that. She was ready to die and her actions showed that. So I was blessed with the thought of everything that she put on me I do to her but give her everlasting peace. "Cathey you are a genius." I love telling myself that. I told myself that at that very moment. So little by little I would sneak around the house when my mother was sleeping and take all sorts of things like knives, liquids, and small tools, and cut pieces of the rope she used to tie me and hide all those things in my room for our big moment or surprise in an essence of my mom's awakening. I do not remember exactly how everything went down but it was a Sunday night my mother had told me before she left the clean the entire house her mess at that.

I responded, "Ok." but I had no intentions of cleaning the house I wanted peace I hated my mom and her fucking peace of shìt house. Moments later I started to knock pictures off the wall, break the glassware around the house, rip apart all the furniture, flooded the bathroom, and punch holes in the wall. I didn't know where my mom was going but I had time. I had so much time that I even destroyed her bedroom and set her most-priced possession in the backyard on fire. As I watched her possessions go in flame a burden upon me was uplifted because all those things reminded me of her. But if they are no longer present my mom would be a memory. I was blessed with another thought that came from someone that was not me. "Kill her." That thought ran through my mind endlessly. It ran through my mind so much that at that moment freedom came and stood next to me and held my hand. I watch the fire burn a little bit longer and then went back into my house and sat in my room waiting for her to get back home.

As I sat there quietly suddenly I hear the door knob moving. The house we stayed in was old and the doors, windows, and certain parts of the floor would make strange noises. I knew it was her. The door finally opened and I hear something drop to the floor. I smiled. My mother was in awe something she had not experienced in a long time. "Cathey Milton!?" She screamed. I didn't respond I smiled harder because she does not know what is going on, where I am, or what I'm thinking.

"Cathey Milton!?" This is going to be my last time calling your name come here now! What the fuck did you do to my house you little whore." My smile then turned into a frown then out of nowhere my rage takes over me.

"You wanna play games with me, don't you? Well, I got a game for us both to play."She said. I chuckled because the game has already started and it was my game we are playing. I hear my mom stepping over things, and knocking things out of her way. I already knew she was coming to my room I hear a particular part of the floor makes the same strange sound. As soon as I heard that she was coming down the hall to my room. I then grab a knife, and a long piece of rope and stood behind my door so that when she walks in I can just jump out and give her the peace she always wanted. As she opens the door she screams, "Where are you fucking whore?" As she walks in she stands directly in the front of my room with her back turned and arms by her side. A voice in my head said, "Get her!" I lunged from behind the door and threw the rope around her neck and took her to the floor. I started to strangle her as she did me when she punished me. But my mom regardless of what I say or anyone says is a fighter and she was not going out without one. As we were on the floor every second I tighten my grip on the rope and each time my mother would groan and fight harder. But I was determined to kill the bitch so I fought harder too. I got the rope as tight as I could around her neck but I was not strong enough to hold it with the same intensity.

As I started to get tired my mother sensed it and began to squirm out of the rope and my arms. Moments later she broke free and I lost grip of the rope and rolled from underneath her. As she tries to get up she is out of breath and turns over on her front side. I stood there in shock because I didn't feel anything or anyone. As my mother lies on the ground she says, "I hope you accomplished whatever you had planned because Cathey your life is over."

Suddenly the fire I started outside I see the flames shooting up intensely through the window. I do not even remember if my mom noticed the fire or not but that fire was a representation of me at that moment. That fire shooting up was what I felt on the inside. As my mother slowly started to raise I grab the knife on the floor behind me lifted my hands as high as I could and swung the knife straight down into the back of my mom's head. It sounded like a sword going through the chest of a warrior. The stab was so perfect it was symmetrical to her head. The tip of the knife went straight through the front of her head and was poking out of the back of her head. The knife was so perfectly placed that it was still while still being in her head.

Her eyes were still open. She deserved it. I knew she was dead. I never got the chance to smile at my mom because she hated my smile and smiling in general. I never knew why but as I held the back of the knife I picked her head up with it as if she was a puppet and smiled at her dead face. She smiled back even though I could not see it. She was at peace and so was I. The fire in the backyard had unexpectedly gone out but the smoke of the fire remained. I was free and peaceful, and now that she is dead I can settle in at home.

But before I could do anything I had to make sure my mom was okay. So I dragged her from my room, through the hallway, into her room. As I began to prepare to tuck her in I realized my mom had never gone to sleep without bathing. So I dragged her into the bathroom, strip her clothes off, and gave her a nice hot bath. It was soothing to clean her up she was beautiful alive but she looked better dead. I bathed her for about an hour found her some good sleeping clothes and put them on her. I had trouble putting her shirt on because I left the knife still in her head. Once I fully dressed her I pull the covers back on her bed, adjusted her pillows, and laid her down softly. The only thing I had trouble with was the placement of her head because the knife looked good going through her head. After I turned her head where I can see both sides of the knife. I stood there in the shambolic room and told my mom, "Goodnight. See you in the morning." I walked out and shut the door behind me.

The next morning came I went to check up on my mom and she was still sleeping peacefully. Now that I am certain she is peaceful I wanted to see how peaceful I could become but the house itself reminded me of my mom and the terrors she brought me. So I started to live in the house inside my head. A house where it was only me and whatever I wanted I could bring to my house. Those things were thoughts that made me feel wanted, and satisfied, and whatever brought unconditional love to me. The things that were not perfect in the physical world I made them perfect in my head. Though I had a mom I made my own mom her name was Nancy, I made dad his name was Hernan, and the house in my head was a lot bigger than the one I lived in. I enjoyed my parents, the house, and myself. My parents were always asking me questions, checking on me, feeding me, and never discipline me as much as my real mom did.

I would be at home all day long until one of my real mom's friends came over one day I think the front door was unlocked and what she witnessed was spine-chilling. I was in my other house with my other mom and dad and I hear a scream and immediately scream, "Mom!" I thought she had woken up from her peaceful rest but it was Mary her long-time friend who was in the room screaming at my mom, "Why did you do this to yourself. I told you I was here for you!! I loved you! You were just hurting. Mary begins to cry harder and notices me out of the corner of her eye. She then said, "where were you Cathey when she did this?" I said, "I was at home. I didn't know mommy was hurting. But I know now that mommy's not hurting anymore. She is at her new home now."

3

The Mirror

She had been dead for quite a while. About two weeks before I killed her she would carry around a green handheld mirror and look into it and say, "I miss the old you. You were so much happier." I never knew who she was referring to until me and Mary's little talk. She was talking about herself. She loved herself too much to lose herself but she did. I also understood why she hated when I smiled, laughed, played, and tried to enjoy myself because she could not. If she could not be happy I could not either. My mom was also a reflection of me.

I was her in her days of joy and when the sorrow can we no longer were a reflection. The only reflection I had of my mom was from looking at myself. So that same mirror she used I kept it for me. That's why I have it now. I'm still talking to and through it as I spill my experiences in existence. This mirror allows me to see various seasons of life during particular times. The same as it did for my mom. But when I look into the mirror my world becomes larger than life. I see my other mom and dad clearer, the house seems bigger, and I enjoy talking and interacting with everything else in my world. I'm the prettiest woman in my world, I have the most money, the most fame, and the best home in my entire world. I'm loved.

Every time my mom adjusted the mirror and I was in the mirror's view she never acknowledged me or punished me she only saw herself and the world inside her head. I knew she had another home another place to go where I was not welcomed. That hurt me. Because I always wanted to be side by side with mommy for some reason. I just did not want to hurt. She took good care of me when she wanted to but other than that fuck her! As far as my father I never knew him he died right after I my birth. He is a pointless thought. Fuck him too! I have my own dad anyway.

After my mom's funeral which was a celebration for me, Mary became my guardian. It was the same as mommy's house just a little different. I had my own room, my own bathroom, my own closet, a radio player, and a bigger mirror. The only difference was that I was not punished at all with Mary. To be frank, Mary felt more like a mom than my mommy did. I knew then I could not be blamed for my mom's severe sadness. Mary always told, "You feel like the daughter I never had. It was meant to be this way." And it was because now I had a mirror for mommy and for my world. The mirror in my room at Mary's house took up a good portion of the wall and I could see half of the room behind me. So what I would do was place mommy's mirror up against the window angled at my face and I sat or stood directly in front of Mary's big mirror.

I remember just having fun in my mind being at home with my parents, and everyone enjoying my presence. The only time I left my mirrors was when it was time to eat, study, or do my weekly chores I stayed in the room almost all day during that time I never went outside, played with others, or even try to make friends I already had friends and family, and I enjoyed playing in my own world. When I look in the big mirror the only vision I had was of my world and in mommy's mirror I saw her laying down with the knife I used to kill her still in her head. She was peaceful and so was I. "A happy ending right Cathey?" Yes, it was at least in terms of me and my mother. Mary was a busy woman she owned a cake shop and spent most of her time there and had neighbors watching the house and looking out for me.

She would often get home after I was asleep she would walk in check on me and get me together every morning before she left. I did not go to school for some time Mary thought it would be better if I took some time off so that every day during that time I had the chance to watch over mommy and be at home with Nancy my other mom my dad Hernan. He was a businessman so he worked a lot just like Mary. He would always say, "I work hard so you do not have to." My mommy never told me that. It was always, "I work hard you work hard." But that's what I loved about my other home everything was the complete opposite. Nancy my other mom was the sweetest woman alive. "I love you" she always said softly I did not hear that from my mom either but it felt good to hear it from someone. It had been three months since mommy passed and throughout those three months I was basically alone except for in the morning when Mary was there.

But one day Mary came home early which I was unaware and my dad and I got into an argument over me talking back. I told him to talk quietly because he could wake mommy up. My dad then said, "you only have one mom!" I shouted back at my dad, "I have two mommies and one daddy! Shut up before you wake up mommy!" Mary burst into my room and says, "who are you talking to?" I heard Mary but I was still gazing in the mirror looking at my dad. I then said, "Take it back dad?" Mary then runs over to me and grabs me intensely. "What's going on? Who are you talking to?" I looked over at Nancy and pointed directly at the center of the mirror and said, "him." Mary looked confusingly and said, "there is nothing there Cathey. Nothing in either mirror but our own reflection." My dad said something as Mary was talking to me and we began to argue again. Mary sat there and watched me until I and my dad's argument was over. It was complete silence until Mary said, "Catherine are you ok?" Mary called me by my mommy's name. I felt disrespected because I was not hurt or suicidal. I did not respond to Mary I just got into bed and laid down. Mary tucked me in and kiss me on my forehead sincerely.

That day she came and laid down in the bed which I assumed she did to comfort me but that was not the case. Before Mary got into the bed she took off all her clothes in front of me placed them by the door pulled back the covers and laid down on the side of me. I tried not to make eye contact with her but Mary's body was a sensation. Clear brown skin, nice hips, Mary had an ass too, and nice juicy lips. I then turned over and gaze into her brown eyes. She started to smile and so did I. I felt Mary's energy and I wanted to match it but I wanted Mary to make the first move.

Mary suddenly breaks the silence and says, "I loved your mom and she loved me. She was part of the reason I wanted to live and now that she is gone. All I have is you. And if your mom didn't tell you we were lovers she just didn't tell you because she didn't know how to or how you would feel." It would not have mattered I would not have understood anyway. My memory of the conversation after that was blurred but I do remember Mary kissing me on the lips. That was my first kiss and it was from the same woman who kissed my mom "supposedly." After she kissed me I started to get nervous or was it adrenaline? Whatever it was I was thrilled. She kissed me again and I kissed her back. It was a hard slow kiss with a little tongue. We begin to kiss harder and Mary abruptly stops and quickly begins to pull my shorts and panty's off. After she does she goes down on me and began making love to my vagina. I screamed not because it was painful but because the pleasure I got from it was heavenly. Mary then slowly began to kiss from my stomach all the way up to my lips. After we met face to face lips to lips I swiftly flipped Mary over and began to make love to her whole body.

"Cathey you know what was so strange about that time you had sex with Mary?" "What Cathey?" You forgot about everything nothing mattered the only thing that mattered was the sensation of pleasure. That was true. I had forgotten about mommy, Nancy, Hernan, and my world. I was in Mary's world a world of thrills. As I and Mary were going at it I saw both my mommy's and daddy watching me. I do not know if they were proud, appalled, or confused but what I do know when I looked over at Catherine our sexual sensation was so powerful she woke up from her peace to witness me have sex for the first time. She was jealous but there was nothing she could do but watch. My other parents were in awe they thought I was perfect but once again they live my world and I'm perfect so what I did was perfect. I was thirteen. A baby. Well not after that. Mary started to kiss me again and I did not see Merritt or my other parents I saw myself and Mary. But truly I saw Catherine. Catherine was me. Catherine was miserable, hurt, and annoying. If Mary was her friend and was open to sleeping with me she is sick and hurt too. "Cathey you are safe." That is what I heard in my head. I was safe once again I was innocent no one could blame me for that. Mary took advantage of me so now it was my turn. But since Mary trusted me I knew I could be patient. "Cathey you a smart bitch!" "I know Cathey thank you."I love telling myself that in mommy's mirror.

Back to what I was saying. I had to be a little patient I wanted this to be a sensation, a thrill, and endearment to my mom's girlfriend. I waited for about two in a half weeks and the time came. I was with my other parents and Mary bursts into my room again. It felt like mommy's house all over again Mary began to punish me and call me out my name. She called me crazy. She would always rant you have no parents, I'm your parent, and the world I lived in was the same world my mom died in. I mean I just could not believe it. So I cut her off as she was ranting I was not listening anyway. I told her, "Come stand in the mirror and tell me what you see." She walked over smoothly and positioned herself in the center of the mirror and stared into it. It was pure silence and a straight focus on the mirror. Out of nowhere, Mary says, "I see myself and I see Catherine." She did not see me at all she only saw mommy which meant I'll have to send her to her. I abruptly left the room and told Mary, "I"m going to get us something to drink." I poured up me and Mary something to drink but what she didn't know was that I crushed a piece of broken glass into shards and put them in one of the cups.

It was a game unlike me and mommy's where I dictated everything the choice was on Mary. I come back into the room swiftly, "have a drink," I said to Mary. She responded, "which cup is mine?" I don't know what you pick." She grabs the cup with glass in it. "It was meant to be this way," I said in my head we took a toast and began to drink and as Mary took her first swallow she began to cough and shortly after started to cough up blood. She hit the floor choking, gasping, for air, and grabbing me tightly as her hand slowly started to roll off my body she was pointing the fuck you finger. She knew. I was surprised but what shocked me even was Mary dying last words to me. "I... I... know you killed your mom. You...fucking....demon. You...?" She died. She died talking shit. As I looked over at mommy's mirror once again Merritt was wide awake from her peaceful sleep to witness me kill her lover. My other parents watched once again in disbelief but what I did was perfection. I gave her a choice of life or death. Mary chose to be with Merritt. Mary chose death.

4

Shattered glass

I kill that bitch too. Oh well. I started to laugh. "I did?" I did it was funny at least for me. I was also a smart bitch. Still am. And I had to cover up my tracks so what I did was chip the glass cup she had and tell whoever comes she made a mistake. She was not paying attention! And she swallowed glass out of her chipped cup. Boom. "Couldn't nobody blame you, Cathey?" Nope. I finished my juice with a smooth swallow. Mary was still laying there and I felt like if she wanted to move she had to do it herself. I never touched her after she died I wanted her to lay there so I can look after her, mommy, and be at home with my parents.

I loved it because the world was mine again. Peaceful everyone saw Cathey for Cathey and I knew myself. Mary was like my mom she didn't have many friends or family at least to my knowledge so I knew I would be able to be there for a while peacefully. But unlike the free time I had at mommy's house this time, I wanted to go all out. Mary smoked cigarettes, drank liquor, and smoked weed sometimes in the morning before she left home. I strip the entire house and found her stash in the wall of her bedroom. It was more than I thought she had weed, cigarettes, liquor, pills, needles, and some other liquids. I only took the liquor, weed, and pills I knew to stay away from that other shit. I do not remember the names of the liquor, didn't know any of the pills, and the weed was good. I remember opening a clear bottle of liquor and taking a sip. It burned my chest as if I drank hot water. Suddenly I felt different as in my body I felt loose. So I wanted to get looser and I chugged a big gulp and remember dropping the bottle on Mary's head and I hit the floor holding my chest as if I was dying. It was short-lived I was okay. At that moment mommy was sitting up watching me laughing. She was only laughing because she thought I was dying.

But I felt like mommy was only paying attention because she was bored, and in the same position as the window. My other parents just watched me in awe once again but they never judged me because I was perfect. Still am! At least I think. With Mary being dead and no one ever coming to the house I had to be sure the neighbors or anyone unexpectedly coming by would not bring or cause any attention to Mary being absent, dead, or something going on within the house. I came across some blank posters and notebooks in Mary's kitchen and I wrote, "Out of town will be back home soon. Thanks." I added other things but that was the most important. I put these "heads-up" messages in the window, on the front door, and the outside the gate of the house. I felt like a genius because no one would think much of it.

Once I put up all the messages I went back into the house to enjoy my freedom and peace. When I got back into the room I screamed, "I'm home! No one gave me a warm welcome the room was at a standstill. Mommy was asleep, Mary was still dead, and my other parents just sat there. I stared into both mirrors and it was nothing. I guess they all wanted a break from me. So, I decided to enjoy my world by myself. I grabbed a bottle of liquor and began to drink it erratically. I admit I didn't know what I was doing but I was doing it. After the second gulp, my head started to spin, my vision started to blur, and my world became more apparent.

When I stared into mommy's mirror all I saw was mommy. Every moment of my existence with mommy I saw it again but it was so fast! Suddenly mommy was right in front of me. I could not believe it. She was smiling, she gave me direct eye contact and she reach out for a hug. I hugged her. That was my first time ever hugging mommy. She then said, "if you need anything ask me. Mommy will always be here." I had a million questions for her but as I opened my eyes to start asking questions she was gone. She was not in front of me nor was she in the mirror. I told myself, "I might be drunk." I was but now that I can't see mommy I was afraid. There is no one watching over or after me. I started to gaze in the big mirror and my other parents came out directly in front of me but their backs were turned. My feelings of being afraid to turn to joy because I have people that will look after me. I said, "Mom!? Dad!? You came to see me!?" My other mother said, "Take my hand and come with us." I stopped and thought about it and said, "What about mommy!?" My other mother said, "I'm your only mom. Now come with me before you get punished!" The word punishment scares me. I cannot remember exactly but I did take a few steps back. Out of nowhere, my other mommy says, "Cathey don't fucking play with me." I was enraged because my other mommy was supposed to be different.

I screamed, "Fuck you! Ya old bitch! Your not my mom!" My other mommy slowly started to turn her head gradually but her body stay in the same position. I was curious to see her face but once her head was fully turned around I was horrified. It was Catherine! It was mommy. Then my dad started to turn his head but it was not my dad it was Mary. "Come on Cathey before mommy gets mad and punishes you." "I'm staying here." It was I told her. "Okay. Fine. Stay here." I didn't respond and in the blink of an eye, she was gone and so was Mary. I can't really remember everything clearly but I had to regain my composure so I just laid down on the bed moments later I was out cold. A few hours after I woke up I scanned the room. Mary was still in the same spot lifeless, mommy was not in her mirror, and neither was my other mommy or dad. Every time I looked into the mirrors I didn't see anything, not even a reflection. I began to look harder. As my concentration heighten I saw mommy just a smaller version.

But this mommy was playful she mimicked every movement, facial expression, and eye contact. She even mimicked the words I was saying. I was confused and in pain but in physical pain from the after-effects of alcohol. In a way, I felt like mommy I was hurt, alone, with no one to turn to. I was mommy's reflection. I walked up to the mirror one last time as close as I could look into the mirror and saw Merritt looking directly at me. "I'm miserable. I am nothing. I am a reflection of you." Then I realize that was not mommy that was me. I'm exactly like mommy something I never wanted to be I hated myself because I was hurt just like mommy and used my head as a way out of my pain. I didn't know or understand anything. Since I hated mommy and did not want anything but her love and she still leaves me. I took the bottle of liquor I drank and throw the bottle as hard as I could at the mirror. It shattered. And in every crevice of the glass, I saw memories of mommy I experienced and portions of her life I never saw before.

In the biggest crevices of the glass, I saw her joyful moments, and in the smaller crevices, I saw her at her lowest. I was blessed with another thought mommy was like a mirror she had a clear vision and image until she shattered and couldn't see herself clearly. It was the same for me at that moment until I heard a voice I don't know if it was in my head, in the house, or outside but heard someone say, "It's all shattered." I said aloud, "How?" It was complete silence but I did know it was shattered.

5

Catherine

All of a sudden I was a grown woman. I was officially Catherine. Cathey had died. I didn't die but Cathey became a memory. I was my mother's twin I had to live with that my whole life even till this day. I can't even remember my childhood after the shattered glass incident. But at that moment I realized I was grown I was on the floor beaten half to death by my husband whom I had never seen until that moment. But was so crazy I knew his name, occupation, his birthday, and even our children's name. I remember him saying "Get the fuck up. Ya dumb bitch." I slowly get up and my husband was "drunk and a skunk." I finally was standing straight up and he knocked me to the floor again. I wanted to fight back but I suffering physically in excruciating pain. As I lay on the floor I hear my children run in Willow and Alexander and my husband beats them too.

Not long after he bathes all of us in the tub together in silence. After he cleaned us he left the restroom and said, "nobody leaves or I'll go crazy." We all stood there naked waiting for him to return. I gazed in the mirror at myself and saw Catherine. "She was looking at me and said, "Now you see. The pain I received from others caused me suffering. I couldn't suffer alone. My name is not Catherine my name is Misery. I will always need company." I hated myself for a moment but I had to accept the fact that I was miserable and addicted to misery. Sickness is an addiction and misery made me sick to my stomach. Not only was I miserable but my children were too. I had to change that. The only way to get out of misery was to kill anything that brought misery.

My husband. I mean I barely knew him but I knew him. I asked myself, "How could someone or something you don't know to bring you much pain and misery?" But I also thought misery is a state of mind. The first step to not being miserable was to accept myself for who I was. I loved myself and I was fine as wine still is. So I had to make a choice. "Do I prefer my safety over my freedom or freedom over my safety?" My freedom and now was the time to act.

I knew Marshall would come back in the bathroom drunk. Marshall was my husband's name. Back to what I was saying I hit him with the simplest move in the book. I walked the kids into the tub and pulled the shower curtain back I then walked and stood behind the door. Suddenly, the door opens and he stumbles in. I didn't even give him a chance to come through the door fully. I just knock him to the floor grab a wooden plank that was in the corner I was standing in. The same plank used to beat us. It was about fifteen inches long and about five pounds. I blacked out. All I remember was hitting him while he was on the floor and in some sort of way he got to his feet and were both fighting for our lives. Already ready suffering a beating and pain I didn't have much energy.

So he ended up overpowering me and knocking me unconscious. As I was on the ground he keep smashing his fist directly in my face. My head was literally bouncing off the ground like a basketball. I hear the curtains of the shower pull back and a draw opening very quickly. As I hear noise in the background every hit got harder and harder. I remember him getting ready to hit me I think for the very last time and he cocked his arm as far as he could and right before it's downward motion my soon Alexander stabbed him in the back of the head with a pair of scissors.

The same way I did Catherine. It was a Deja-vu. My husband fell over and my son was helping me up. Alexander. That was my baby. That was my boy. He killed his dad. He hated misery which means he would have hated Catherine. That's fine with me. My daughter Willow was sitting there smiling she hated misery too. That filled me up with joy so I cut the bath water back on filled the tub up and we played in the tub all night. We even cleaned daddy up for the first time. That was also his first time bathing with us. Marshall had fun I even let Willow play with him for a while. Kind of a sexuality experiment. She liked her father she even did a few tricks on him. Alexander was just slapping the shit out of him smack in the face. Daddy didn't get angry, yell, or even talk back. For the first time, he was being a respectful and responsible parent.

After our family bath, we all went to lie down. Alexander wanted to sleep with me and Willow wanted to sleep with her daddy. Willow had her own room so she cried to have daddy with her. He needed to spend time with her anyway so we drag him into her room, put him in the bed, and positioned him the way she insisted he be. We finished and I walked out of the room. I walked into my bedroom or our bedroom and Alexander was still naked waiting on me. For some odd reason, I was thrilled, nervous, and excited because although he was a child I did not know his wisdom but I knew he was beyond his years.

That was the only moment I vividly remember with my children. But, their faces are always in my head and occasionally in my mirror. Oh, that's right my mirror! Let me look into my mirror! Aww, Fuck! Catherine! Catherine! I fucking hate seeing you. I hate seeing my mother, and she is looking back at me mimicking, my every moment, look, and expression. She's lucky I love her enough to not break her mirror. But, just because the mirror provides a clear reflection does not mean the person looking into it is shattered.

II

The Angelic Note

*Everyone loves to call Cathey crazy! The hell with
them I remember Mary telling me after my mom died,
"there is a place for people like you. You will send
yourself there." I think she was talking about insanity.
I'm not insane anyway if I was I would have figured
that out years ago. Though the only thing I never may
know is who knows me more than I do.
Let me look into the mirror to see my life story so I can
tell my story. "It's shattered." Cathey, who said that?
I don't know. The mirror. Mom?*